Animal Fun Facts

# FUN FACTS ABOUT BATS

by Julie Murray

Dash!

LEVELED READERS

2

An Imprint of Abdo Zoom • abdobooks.com

**Dash!**
**LEVELED READERS**

**Level 1 – Beginning**
Short and simple sentences with familiar words or patterns for children who are beginning to understand how letters and sounds go together.

**Level 2 – Emerging**
Longer words and sentences with more complex language patterns for readers who are practicing common words and letter sounds.

**Level 3 – Transitional**
More developed language and vocabulary for readers who are becoming more independent.

THIS BOOK CONTAINS RECYCLED MATERIALS

**abdobooks.com**

Published by Abdo Zoom, a division of ABDO, PO Box 398166, Minneapolis, Minnesota 55439.


Printed in the United States of America, North Mankato, Minnesota.
052021
092021

Photo Credits: Alamy, iStock, Science Source, Shutterstock
Production Contributors: Kenny Abdo, Jennie Forsberg, Grace Hansen, John Hansen
Design Contributors: Candice Keimig, Neil Klinepier

**Library of Congress Control Number: 2020919486**

**Publisher's Cataloging in Publication Data**

Names: Murray, Julie, author.
Title: Fun facts about bats / by Julie Murray
Description: Minneapolis, Minnesota : Abdo Zoom, 2022 | Series: Animal fun facts | Includes online resources and index.
Identifiers: ISBN 9781098224448 (lib. bdg.) | ISBN 9781098225384 (ebook) | ISBN 9781098225858 (Read-to-Me ebook)
Subjects: LCSH: Bats--Juvenile literature. | Bats--Behavior--Juvenile literature. | Nocturnal animals—Behavior--Juvenile literature. | Questions and answers--Juvenile literature. | Animal behavior--Juvenile literature.
Classification: DDC 599.4--dc23

# Table of Contents

# Fun Facts About Bats

There are more than 1,300 bat **species** throughout the world. More than 40 species live in the United States.

Bracken Cave in Texas is home to the largest bat **colony** in the world. Around 20 million bats **roost** here each year.

Bats are the only mammals that can fly! Their wings can work like human arms and hands.

# Homologous Structures

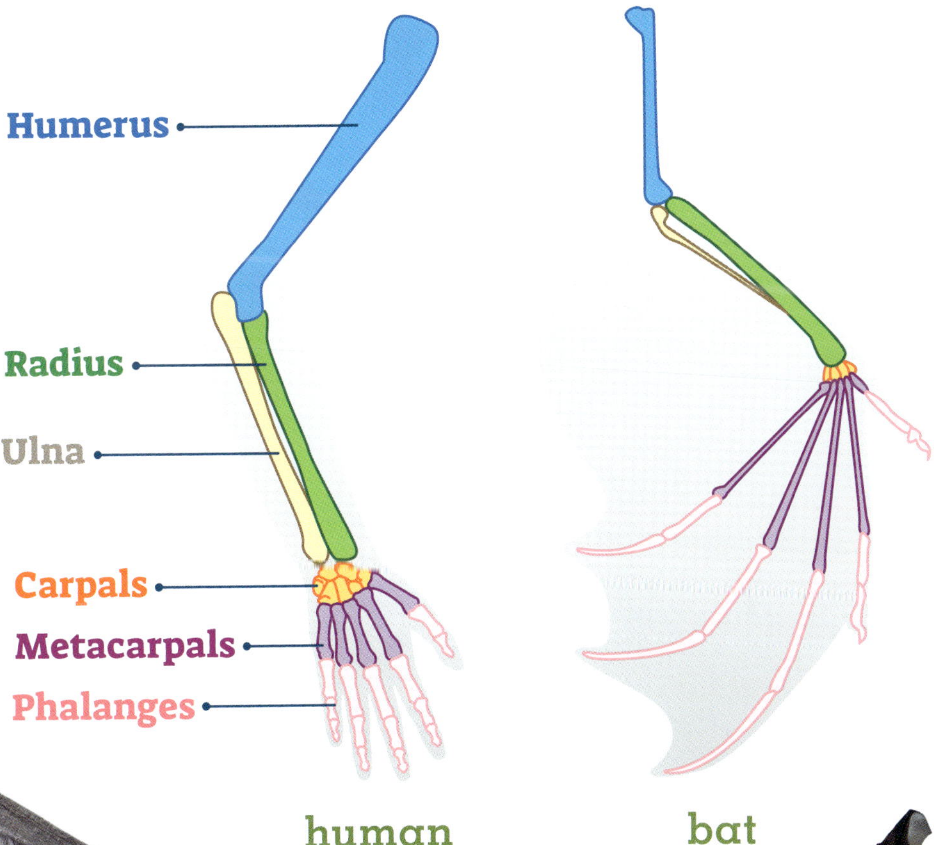

The Brazilian free-tailed bat is the fastest-flying bat. It can fly 100 miles per hour (161 kph)!

Bats help forests stay healthy. Many kinds of plants rely on bats for **pollination**. Bats also help spread seeds.

Many bats eat insects. Some bats will eat 1,000 insects per hour!

Vampire bats, like their name suggests, feed on blood! They **prey** on animals like cows and horses. They sometimes prey on humans too!

The smallest bat **species** is the Kitti's hog-nosed bat. It is just 1 inch (2.5 cm) long. Because of its size, it is also called the bumblebee bat.

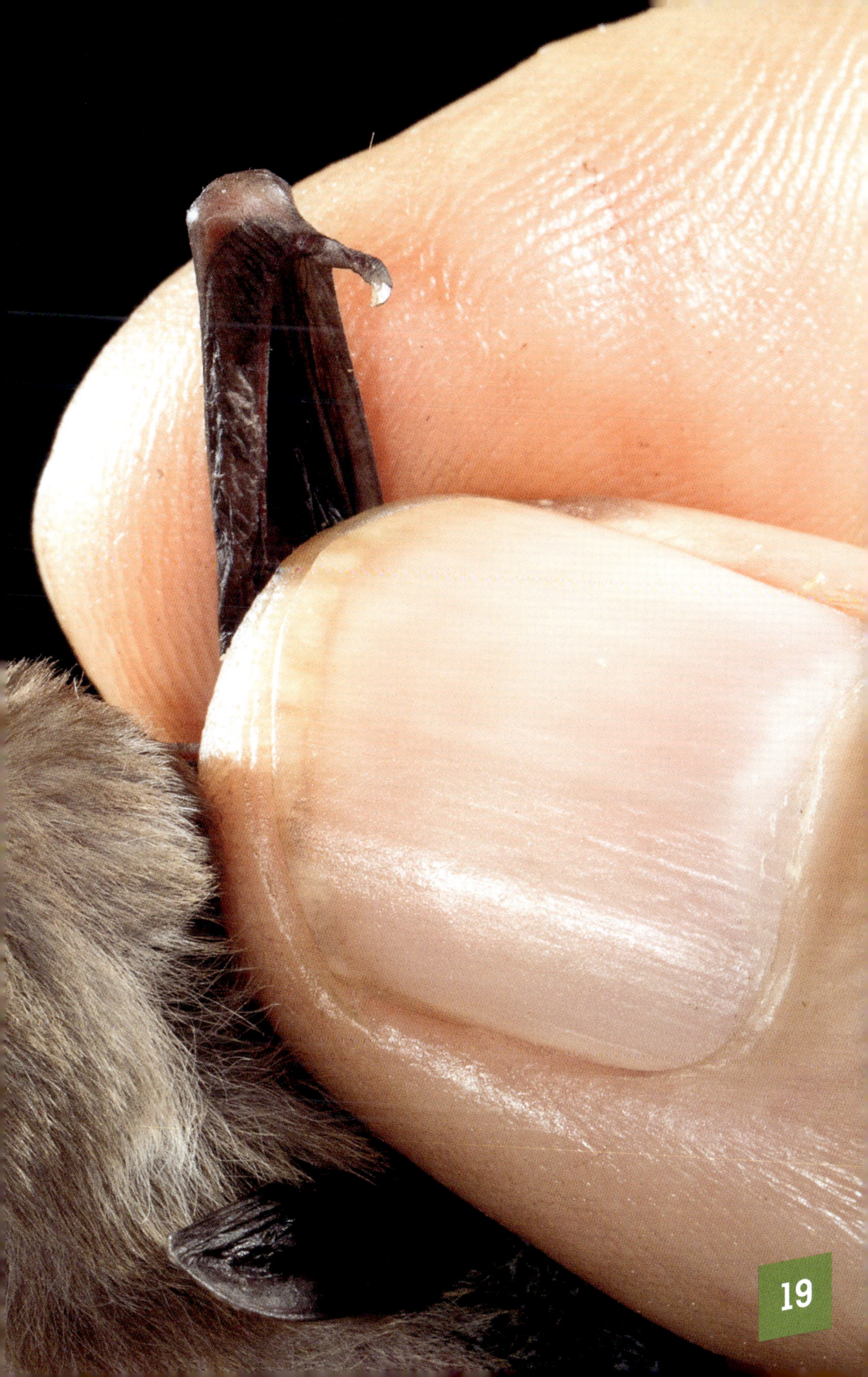

The largest kinds of bats are flying foxes. There are around 60 different **species**. Flying foxes can be found in South and Southeast Asia, Australia, and East Africa.

# Animal Spotlight

## Hoary Bat

**Size**: 5 to 6 inches (12.7-15.24 cm) long; Up to 1.23 ounces (35 g)

**Wingspan**: 15.5 inches (40 cm)

**Appearance**: brown with white-tipped hairs, short ears, and large teeth.

**Range**: North America, Central America, South America

**Habitat**: woodlands, forests, caves

**Diet**: insects; favors moths

# Glossary

**colony** – animals of the same species living closely together.

**pollination** – the transfer of pollen to allow for fertilization.

**prey** – to hunt, catch, and eat another animal.

**roost** – to land or rest on a roost, which is a perch on which bats rest or sleep.

**species** – a group of living things that look alike, share a common name, and can have young with one another.

# Index



# Online Resources

Booklinks
NONFICTION NETWORK
FREE! ONLINE NONFICTION RESOURCES

To learn more about bats, please visit **abdobooklinks.com** or scan this QR code. These links are routinely monitored and updated to provide the most current information available.